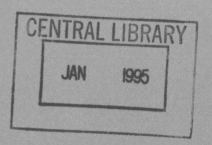

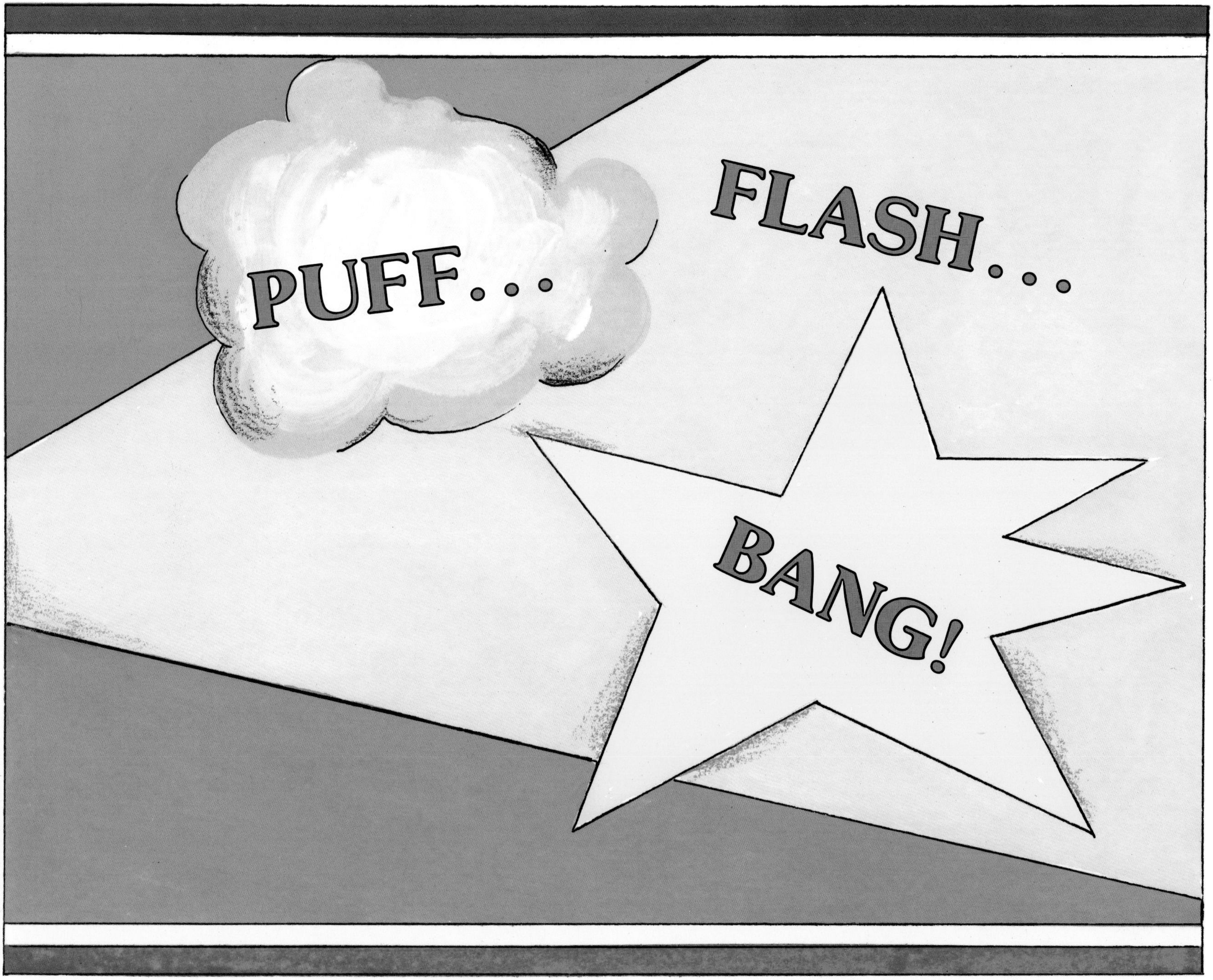
PUFF...
FLASH...
BANG!

PUFF...

A Book About Signals

FLASH...

BANG!

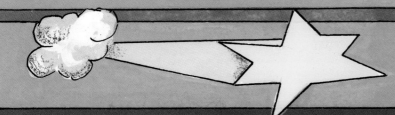

Gail Gibbons

Morrow Junior Books New York

For Olis Thurston

Watercolors, colored pencils, and India ink were used for the full-color artwork. The text type is
16-point Souvenir.

Printed in Hong Kong by South China Printing Company (1988) Ltd.
1   2   3   4   5   6   7   8   9   10

Library of Congress Cataloging-in-Publication Data
Gibbons, Gail.
Puff...flash...bang! : a book about signals / Gail Gibbons.   p.   cm.
    Summary: Describes ways people say things to each other without using spoken or written words
such as beacon fires, hand signals, alarms, and flags.
ISBN 0-688-07377-8 (trade).—ISBN 0-688-07378-6 (library)
1. Signs and symbols—Juvenile literature.   [1. Signs and symbols.]   I. Title.
P99.G485   1993   302.2'22—dc20   92-13170   CIP   AC

The traffic light turns red. A church bell bongs. The police-car siren
screams. A football referee throws both arms above his head. All of these
are signals.

People use signals to say things to each other without using spoken or written words. We see...

or hear most signals.

Thousands of years ago...

Ancient Romans set fires on mountaintops or on hills to send different messages over long distances. These fires are called beacon fires. One beacon fire signals to ships that there are dangerous cliffs nearby.

On the flatlands, a fire warns waiting troops that the enemy is fast approaching.

Later in time, and in another part of the world, people use drums to send messages. A tribesman beats out a signal to nearby villages saying there is to be a great feast.

Horns are used to make signals, too. On a Viking ship a horn blasts its warning to soldiers on shore. A raiding party is coming!

Across the ocean...

A Native American quickly pulls a blanket off a damp, smoking fire. A puff of smoke rises up toward the sky, telling people that the harvest is about to begin. The number of puffs changes depending on the signal.

Other Native Americans use columns of smoke for signals. One column of smoke means "Pay attention!" Two columns of smoke mean "All is well." Three columns of smoke... "Danger!"

During the American Revolution, soldiers use cannon as signals. The cannon are spaced miles apart. The first one is fired. Its sound travels to the next group of soldiers. They fire their cannon. Then a third burst sounds. And a fourth cannon fires. This is a loud relay of cannon bursts signaling that all troops must advance.

Meanwhile, Paul Revere plans a signal to warn the people of Boston that British troops are going to attack. He waits on horseback while a friend watches from a tall church belfry. Lanterns will be the signal. One lantern means the British are coming by land...two lanterns, by sea. Two lanterns shine! Paul Revere makes his famous ride, shouting the warning.

Today, many signals are sight signals.

stop
caution
BLINK!
go

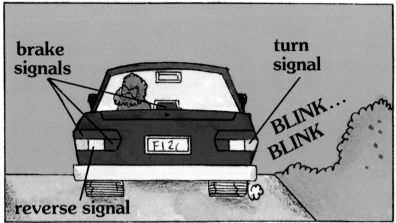

brake
signals
turn
signal
BLINK...
BLINK
reverse signal

headlights

Lights are signals we see every day. Some cars stop at the intersection and others go. A traffic light tells the drivers what they should do.

Cars have light signals, too. They have turn signals, brake signals, and bright and dim headlights for other cars and trucks to see.

At the railroad crossing, a sign blinks off and on. Cars and trucks come to a stop. The signal warns them not to cross the track because a train is coming.

Light signals are used to guide boats and ships through seaway systems. The flashing lights make different patterns. They tell the ships' crews when they can proceed through a lock or a canal and when they should stop.

Out at sea, the captain of a ship looks for a flashing light. It is a lighthouse beacon. Like the beacon fires of old, the lighthouse warns the captain that his ship is near the rocky coast. Each lighthouse flashes its own signal. Lighthouses guide ships and boats safely from one place to another.

Flares are other sight signals. They are used to signal for help. At the side of a highway a car breaks down. The driver places a flare next to her car and waits for help.

A ship is in danger at sea. The crew signals another boat by shooting a flare into the dark sky.

Often, mirrors are used to send signals, too. A camper climbs to a hillside and reflects the light off the surface of her mirror. This tells her distant companion where she can be found.

"Finish!"

"Require assistance!"

"S"

Flags are also used for signaling. Some flags show their meaning through color and design. A race car zooms by! A checkered flag signals to the driver that he has completed the race.

A ship can use flags to send messages to other ships. Each flag signals a different message.

Sometimes the way flags are moved gives their signal. A Boy Scout moves two flags into different positions to signal letters of the alphabet to a friend. This is called semaphore signaling. When one flag is used, it is called wigwagging.

"Hush!"

"Time out!"

"Lower the boom!"

People use hand signals, too. Some hand signals are known all over the world. A parent signals to her child to quiet down.

During a football game, the referee signals the players to stop. The two teams must wait for a decision to be made on a play. Then the game can start again.

The noise in the steel mill is very loud. The workers wear headgear to protect their ears. One worker signals another worker to pick up a heavy beam.

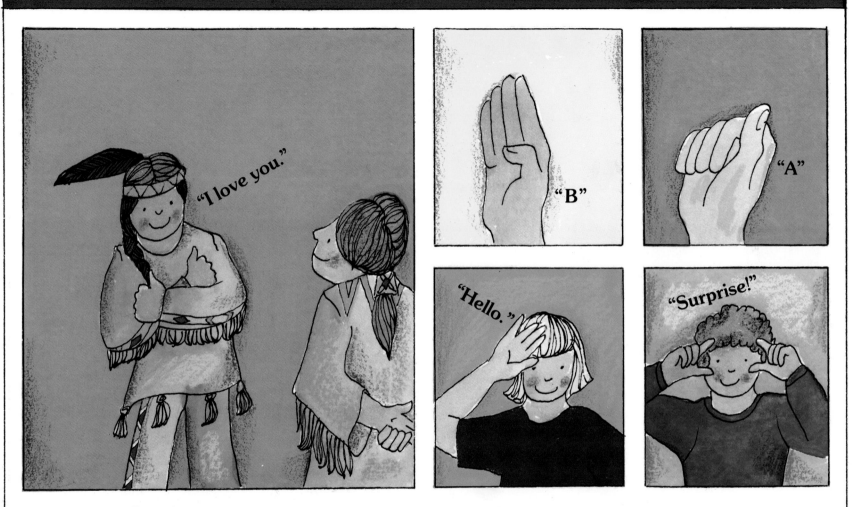

Sign language is a system of hand signals. Sign language has been used for a very long time. American Indians used sign language when they didn't speak the same language.

Today, many deaf people use sign language to communicate. They may signal an entire word or they may spell the word using their fingers.

There are many kinds of sound signals.

A whistle is a sound signal. A woman whistles for her dog to come home.

On a playground, the teacher blows her whistle.

In the distance, a train whistle wails. "Stay off the track!" it warns.

Sirens are warning sound signals. A fire-engine siren screams down the road, warning cars and trucks to get out of the way.

Bells are sound signals, too. We hear them all day! It's early morning.
An alarm clock signals that it's time to get up.

The school bell rings. It's the beginning of a school day.

A church bell rings twelve times, telling people that it's noon.

Someone presses the front doorbell to signal "Open the door."

A telephone rings.

In a theater lobby, a soft chime tells the audience that the concert is about to begin.

Sometimes bells are used as warning signals. Then they are called alarms. A fire alarm rings at the firehouse. There's a fire in town! The firefighters rush to their fire engines.

A burglar alarm goes off in a home, signaling the police. They race in their cars, hoping to catch the thief.

Bells are used as safety signals, too. On a foggy night, a harbor bell
buoy rings to guide captains and their crews into the snug harbor.

Horns are used for another kind of signal. In this faraway castle, a celebration is about to begin. Horns announce the arrival of guests.

On the expressway, traffic is backed up. Drivers beep their horns to signal "Let's get moving!"

At summer camp, a horn signals that it's time to get up.

Guns are fired to signal the beginning of some races. People at the swimming meet hold their breaths. A gun is fired and swimmers dive into the water. They're off!

DOT...DOT...

"Save Our Ship!"

The most widely used sound signal is Morse code. It was invented by Samuel Morse to send messages by electric telegraph. Morse code is a combination of dots and dashes—or short and long sounds—that stand for letters of the alphabet. SOS is an international distress signal—three dots, three dashes, and three dots.

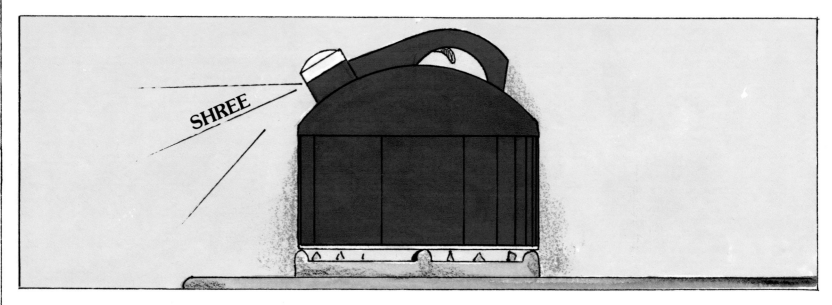

A teakettle whistles. The doorbell rings. A traffic arrow flashes green.

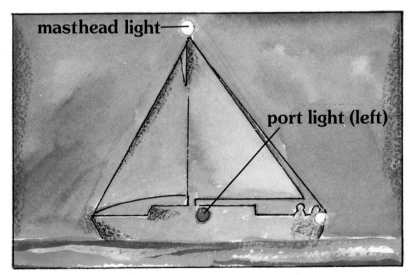

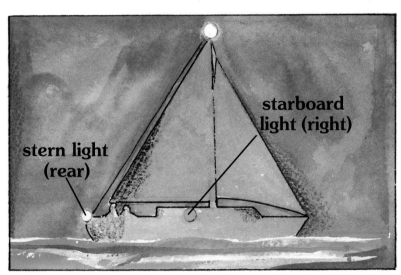

A bell buoy clangs. An airport worker uses batons to guide an airplane into position. Lights tell a boat's direction in the night.

All of these are signals that tell us something we want to know.